APES OF WRATH

For Heather

Also by Steve Bell

Unspeakable If...
Unstoppable If...
Bell's Eye: Twenty Years of Drawing Blood
If... Bottoms Out
The If... Files

by Steve Bell and Brian Homer

Chairman Blair's Little Red Book

Steve Bell

APES OF WRATH

'Man like **monkey** in a **tree**.
Higher he **climb** more **arse** you see.'

Traditional Papua New Guinean saying

methuen

in association with

The Guardian

1 3 5 7 9 10 8 6 4 2

Published in 2004 by Methuen in association with *The Guardian*

Copyright in the text © 2004 Steve Bell

Copyright in the illustrations
© 1988, 1991, 1998, 1999, 2000, 2001, 2002, 2003, 2004 Steve Bell

The right of Steve Bell to be identified as author of this work has been asserted by him in accordance with the Copyright, Designs and Patents Act 1988

A CIP catalogue record for this book is available from the British Library

ISBN 0 413 77450 3

Methuen Publishing Ltd
215 Vauxhall Bridge Road, London SW1V 1EJ
Methuen Publishing Limited Reg. No. 3543167
www.methuen.co.uk

Design by homer**creative**

Printed in China

Im askin you all to **git up outa your seats...**

I got the call from the Reverend Billy Graham on accounta I was born for **higher things** an the **Lord** was askin me to **climb trees**. He gimme long arms and **strong fingers** to git places my Daddy never dreamed. My arms grew **longer** an my walk an talk grew **stronger**. I swore off booze and **took up bananas** on accounta a fuzzy head an **the double vision thing** is no use to a man **swingin from a creeper**. You cant sniff the breeze with a nose fulla **cocaine** and why babble like a **retard** when you got a job **speakin english**?

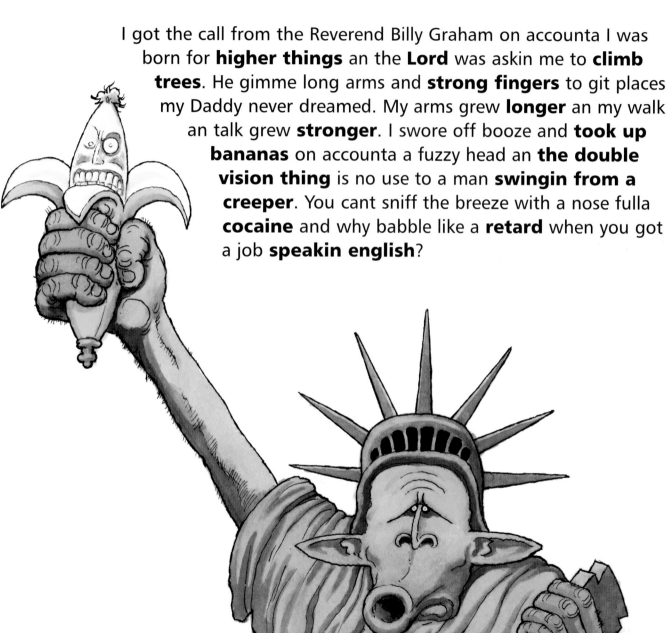

I aint real **smart** I aint good-lookin and I dont **talk good** but I got somethin that people like on accounta Im a **good-time guy** an Im smart enough to know I **aint that smart** but I **know it** which is a lot more smart than most folks who is not that smart also I got guys to **be smart for me** when I need it which is **real smart** an there aint no such thing as **dumb luck** you gotta know how to **use it** when it comes your way

.1.8.00. ©Steve Bell 2000

What made me a **big shot**? I come from a **dynasty** like the **Queen of England** though mine is no way near as old as the **Von Windsorburgs**. I know life at the top on accounta I is the son of a **President** and he is the son of a **Senator**. My granpa was Prescott Sheldon Bush or **Pop** who built up the **Bush family fortune** an showed us the way in politics an who knowed **money** on accounta like hed say if you git the money the rest is gonna **follow on** so dont knock it on accounta it **aint easy** to come by an its darn **easy to lose** an hed cuff me good an call me his lil **strength thru joy** boy

9

Pop put together the **finance for the fewer** back in the early days. He figured that If the fewerd got rid of **communism** before wurl war two there wouldna been any **wurl war two** but there was an Pop got in **big trouble** when they said he was **tradin with the enemy** which aint fair on accounta he was keepin his eye on the **real** enemy the **godless communists**. A lotta dough got froze plus he sent **Poppy** off to fight the Japs become a war hero and flirt with communism. Poppy got voted President back in **88** after bein Veep for eight years under **Reagan**. He had a younger jerk called **Dan Quayle** as his Veep though I got more **family appeal** than him an I say the mercan people **like family**

'AMERICAN SURREAL.' or a Right Pair of Bums ——— AFTER GRANT WOOD

Poppy was smart an knew it which was **less smart** an he thought he was smart enough to **flirt with communism** but nobody **but nobody** is that smart. I respec my Poppy and when folks attack him they is attackin me and I dont like bein attacked on accounta Im not a **forgive and forget** kind of guy like Poppy on accounta I is a Texican. I was born in New Haven Connecticut but I aint a **Yankee** on accounta I was brought up in **Texas** where the horizons is big the hats is big an people walk **tall** speak **slow** talk **straight** live **clean** an dont like to be **messed with**. I tried followin the ol mans footsteps but **his way** was not **my way**. He was a star at **sports** but my eyes is too close together for real good **ball control**. He was a **A student** but Cs was more my style. He was a **war hero** a navy flyer in the Pacific but I never ever saw no action with the **Texas National Guard**. Poppy was a successful **businessman** but I was a no count **fratboy** till I heard the call

Poppy won the **cold war** and the war where he **kicked Saddams ass** but the mercan people only give a shit about payin **too much tax**. He made a big strategical mistake when he said – **Read my lips no new taxes!** on accounta he brought in some new taxes then got beat in **92** by one of the **cheesiest cacters** in mercan politics theres ever been **Bill Clinton**. The guy had no **curge** to do the necessary to git rid of ol Saddam. He was happy to throw bombs in from on high mostly timed to **fool** the mercan people about his evildoins with **Miss Monica Lewinsky** in the oval orifice but he didnt have the **curge** to send some of our boys in **on the ground**. He had no curge no morls and most especially no **morl curge** which is the most important kind

© Steve Bell 1998

· 1068 · 19 · 2 · 98 ·

15

His good **strong ally** was a man of **cacter** and of **curge** more important a man with **morl curge** to do what was right **Primester Tony Blair** of Great Britain England. Tony Blair also come from a big shot dynasty his mother was **Lady Margaret Thatcher** and his father was **Sir Winston Churchill** who won wurl war two and who said that **never** was so much owed by so many to **the fewer** which is somethin we could all learn from. Sir Winston was also a great Yurpeen inventor of the **iron curtain** and lifelong foe of **communism**

Yurp old and noo has been one o my **big ideas** in politics. The **noo yurp** is the best things to have come out of yurp like Sir Winston Churchill Lady Margaret Thatcher and Primester Tony Blair like **freeman moxy** and eurodisney but other stuff like communism evildoers cheap steel imports and the yurpeen union is the **ol yurp**. Lady Margaret Thatcher fought the **yurpeen union** all her life some say it drove her nuts but her work lives on through Primester Tony Blair an the **Britisher Empire** which ruled the wurl way back in ancient times an brought freeman moxy type values and the **Queen of England** to ever country on earth. It was a empire where the sun never set except at night which is how it should be and it curb the power of the **fuzzy wuzzies** who at that time was the **big threat** to mankind comin outa **Fanistan**. Sound familiar?

19

Clinton served **two terms** while I was makin it as a businessman in **oil** and then in **baseball** where I bought up the **Texas Rangers** which got me known as a **straight dealin** kinda guy around **Texas** where I stood for governor in **94**. I won not on accounta **Poppy** but on accounta my secret weapon my **pet fat guy Karl**. Karl knows everthin there is to know about pollin swing votes **bedrock bread and butter issues** all that kinda stuff that bores me shitless but makes or breaks elections. Hes also real good at playin dirty while Im real good at **lookin clean**. Also the poor sap wants to be me except hes too **fat** too **smart** and too **creepy** to ever stand a hope in hell of bein elected **anywhere**

CLINTY WINTY COMES CLEAN

21

In november **2000** I fought Clintons Veep **Al Gore**. I seen dead trees with more appeal than that boy. The oval orifice blow job king kept a **low profile** which was good for me on accounta while Clinton cacterwise is a lyin cheatin evil piece of dirt hes a **damn good campaigner**. Al Gore campaigns like a plank in a sawmill. My only worry durin the campaign was when dull boy gave his wife **Dumpster** a full tongue deep throat french kiss on national prime time. If he coulda pretended to **be human** for a little longer he woulda won easy

So it ran to a tie which Jeb and Karls **contacts** kinda swang our way in **Florda** an Mom said later **Thank Fox for that!** Karls good contacts with **Fox** made sure they was **callin Florda for us** before theyd even voted. That made the big difference since it put dull boy on the back foot which was mainly **smart boy Karls** doin

ELECTILE DYSFUNCTION

23

So I got the **big job** the one Poppy let go in **92**. He was pleased everone was pleased even poor ol Ron Reagan was pleased though he was **never my fren** havin sent guys to fuck me when I first tried runnin for **Congress**. Folks sometimes compare me to him on accounta my great **people skills** but this pisses me since the guy is clearly **dumb as shit** and always was. The guy was a actor an **mouthpiece** for some real cheesy Califiornia businessmen. **Star Wars** was a good idea though and he faced down the commies so I guess I kinda carry the flag now the guy cant even **zip his pants** anymore

I had a **strong team** lined up for the noomercansentry with **Dick** my Veep **Rummy** and **Wolfie** at defense plus **Condi** and **Colin** who is a major league dullard an low grade communist but is a **minordy guy** and mostly does what hes told. Problem is he wants to be president for himself only his wife wont let him on accounta **death threats** from people who should know better

Condi **looks good** period. Better still she impresses dumbshit liberal voters with my track record on **minordy interests** which is a crock of shit unless you is a Texican oil-ownin **rightwing millionaire** minordy plus shes smart and takes the pressure off Laura

With Primester Blair I carried on the low level bombin work on **araq** that had begun under Clinton but it left me **unsatisfied**. I needed to avenge Poppy. I knew Primester Tony Blair was a true **neecon** at heart even though he was leader of the **Britisher communist party**. I admired his **morl curge** and his relationship with **Jesus** and he understood my need to **git Saddam** from day one. I wanna be known as the **energy president** on accounta my deep knowledge of the **oil industry** an my belief in alternative energy sources which is why I invaded **araq**. I also wanna be known as the guy who **put the wurl straight** from communist takeover of wurl energy by **kyoto** who is a forn evildoer of the worst kind

At my nogration as president I pledged to operate a **forn-handed** forn policy which means I leave forn affairs to forners on accounta I mainly aint goin **abroad** durin my presidency. The way I figure it why have a **passport**. We have everthin we need right here like high mountains and cold tundra as well as **Florda** which is pretty damn hot. I been to south merca but thats still merca so goin to **yurp** for the first time in May 2001 was a **big problem**. We landed Airforce One in Spanecia on accounta I can speak the language which you kinda gotta do in Texas to keep in with the spic vote there was a little bitty **diplocrap** an some **evildoer protests** about star wars an kyoto. Havin a passport is a sure sign of **turrism** and I was a lert and vigilant to the dangers of turrism from **day one** of my presidency

31

On accounta my constant lertness to the dangers of terrrsm **911** was no big surprise to me. I was in a school in **Florda** askin the question – **is our children learnin?** like I do ever day of my presidency when they told me what was goin on. I narrowed my eyes. **We was at war**. The first thing I had to do was git to a deep hole in **Nebraska** and wait for **Dick** to call on accounta he knows what to do. Who done it? It was **forners**. For too long the Clinton presidency had been soft on forners so forn evildoers decided to hit us **hard** in the **homeland**. They made a big mistake. **Im no Bill Clinton**. Aside from my pledge never to have sex in the oval orifice I have **no problem** about puttin boots on the ground. Those folks would be hearin from me **real soon**

I narrowed my eyes some more and I was **commander in chief**. Smartasses quit laughin at me on accounta now Im a **wurlstatesman** not just some small time **fratboy**. They laughed at me when I told em about **son of star wars.** They not laughin now

The weekend after 911 I met up with my fren Tony and he stood shoulder to shoulder an gave me a bust of **Sir Winston Churchill**. I gave him a **bomber jacket** and he swore on the **bones of geronimo** to to be my special guy for as long as it takes

35

Our **secret guys** told me they were sure as shittin it was **Osama Bin Laden** a old family friend who was now hangin out in **Fanistan** which is way out east. The mercan people wanted me to **do somethin** about that so I wasn gonna disappoint em. The problem was noone knew where Fanistan was or even if it was **bombable**

37

The **television** which is evil guys with beards that **run Fanistan** an harbor Bin Laden were startin to feel worried so we had em where we wanted em which was in Fanistan and not attackin the **homeland** which we was busy makin safe with the **patriot act** an all

Turns out Fanistan is surrounded by a whole bunch of **other Stans** which meant a whole new round of **diplocrap** to get em to let us bomb Fanistan from ther territory. Mostly they was willin on accounta they like **uncle dollar** an this is where I had a **great idea** I said to Dick – **Let the first bombs be food**. He looked at me like I was nuts which is normal for Dick but then I said – First we confuse em then we can bomb them back into **responsible nationhood** and stop em harborin ol Bin Laden

These days war is like goin to see the doctor – its **mainly surgical**. Bombs is a helluva lot **cleaner** than they was in wurl war one an two an a well placed bomb can mean the difference between **life and death** for a family tryin to **scratch a livin** from some bankrupt dustheap like Fanistan. Its called **improvin the infostatcher** which is somethin Dicks boys at Halliburton do **real good**

41

Fanistan is a country where you hafta watch just **one channel** of TV whether you want to or not or get your **hands chopped off** and where **chicks** hafta walk around in **bags** and say what a great guy **Bin Laden** was to harbor. Turns out he was away on holiday but we fucked the **television** real well and got the **babes outa the bags** in time for christmas

We brought a end to the rule of the television with the **nornlions** who is guys with beards that like to **raise hell** and like **uncle dollar** even more. It worked out kinda neat on accounta they supplied the **boots on the ground** while we supplied the bombs which I was pledged to not like **Clinton** who just liked **poundin dirt for show**

JOHN SIMPSON FLINGS OFF HIS BEARD AND HIS BURQA AS THE BBC SINGLE HANDEDLY LIBERATES...

KABUL IS SO BRACING

By now our **secret guys** plus General Dustin and his warlord guys had been pickin up **terrrsts** and takin em prisoner only we didnt have nowhere to put em so I suggested **shavin ther asses** and puttin em in a cage on accounta it never done me no harm back in **Midland** only the good folks there wouldnt like havin **terrrsts in ther backyard** so we sent em to **Cuba**. There was a incident when terrrsts put **choky sauce** in my pretzel bowl which made me bang my head some so I gave myself a **purple heart** and got on with the job

Mission accomplished meant it was time to go for the real enemy **Saddam Hussein** the **super turrst** the guy who tried to **kill my daddy** sittin there in ol Araq with his massive weapons and his **links to Algator**

Then I found out the **yurpeens** had been floodin the USA with **cheap steel** I had to act fast or look like a wuss that dont give a shit about our **rusty belt people** which I dont on accounta they vote democrat anyway but Karl said I should start worryin about the **mid terms** so I slapped on some **steel turrfs** then sat back an watched them ol yurpeens squealin which was **kinda fun**

47

Although primester Tony Blair is head of the britisher communist party he believes in the **noomercansentry** and how were gonna clean up the wurl for **Jesus** which is somethin he learnt from his momma Lady Margaret Thatcher and his poppa Sir Winston Churchill. I like to call him **my fren Tony** on accounta his cacter and his curge and specially his **morl curge**

49

In the **mideast** the moozlums is **mainly airbs**
except in Isreal where the moozlums is **mainly
jews** except the **terrrsts** who follow the evildoer
Yosser Airfat who like to **blow emselves to shit**.
Since we gotta peacify the mideast I invented the
roadmap which is to show **Areal Shroan** primester
of Isreal where to go to keep the peace which is
wherever he wants on accounta hes spearheadin the
worn terrr

51

One thing I learned since I became president of the Nicedaysmerca is that the **yurpeens** is mainly **chickenshit** and that the **French** is the **most chickenshit** of all the yurpeens which is sayin somethin

© Steve Bell 2002 ~ 1750·23·4·02·

53

The first task of the noomercansentry was to **whack araq** which got kinda delayed on accounta havin to whack Fanistan first which wasnt in the **original plan**. By this time folks was beginnin to forget about **911** so we started to build a collition to git ol Saddam but the **nine asians** was bein chickenshit all round like France

WE MUST **PREEMPTIVELY** **KILL** THIS GUY BEFORE WE CAN **SELL HIM** ANY MORE WEAPONS!

©Steve Bell 2002 – 1774·18·6·02·

SEAL OF THE PRESIDENT OF THE UNITED STATES

Back home there were big problems about our
businesses bein infiltrated by **Enronis** who is
xylophone seekers from Enronistan a evildoer state
out east and part of the **axle of elvis**. I took firm
action to stop this helped by my fren and adviser top
anti-enroni expert **Ken Lay**

CORPORATE
RESPONSIBILITY

SEAL OF THE PRESIDENT OF THE UNITED STATES OF AMERICA

Turns out ol Bin Laden was on holiday in **Bali** which is way way out east not in **Tora Bora** where we was bombin him. He was **bombin surfers** from australia which was even more of a good reason to **hit araq** on accounta if hes gonna show up in Bali then he could just as easy **show up in araq** as anyplace else

59

As time went on my statcher as **war leader** grew.
Folks who used to laugh at me for bein a no account
booze hound fratboy began to sit up and take
notice as I worked to build the **innational collition**
against ol Saddam

© Steve Bell 2002 — 1840·7·11·02 —

61

At the same time the statcher of the **Von Windsorburg dynasty** was goin the other way on accounta some **butler guys** blabbin about takin it up the ass from the **ear to the Queen**

We knew that Saddam possessed **dubyemdee**. This was a terble machine designed to suck the brains out of the Saddam regimes opponents with a **massive tube** made of **yellowcake.** The nine asians sent some creepy fat guy **Hons Blix** to find it but he kept lookin in the **wrong place** on accounta he was too **fat** and too **chickenshit**

Primester Tony Blair told me at this time that one of the things that worries **britisher folks** the most is the **gun culcha** which is on accounta **drug guys** drivin around and blowin people away. I told him about the **NRA** which is what we use to control gun culcha here on accounta if **everbodys got a gun** nobodys gonna be afraid of no **gun culcha**

Then I made my **state o the union** speech about how ol Saddam was buildin **dubyemdee** from yellowcake which Primester Tony Blairs secret guys swore was supplied by **Nigereria** one of the nine asians

One of Primester Tony Blairs **finest features** is the way he can speak in long words mainly in the **right order**. He is a powerful performer when he speaks on accounta his **young confident tone** so you think he really **believes** all the stuff he talks like when he asked what it would be like to **wake up** and find wed all been **blown to shit** by ol Saddam and his **dubyemdee**

69

The only thing I really care about apart from my family my country and Jesus is **freeman moxy** which is why I wanna bring it to araq. People tell me there is **oil** there which I guess is **real good news** for the araqi people as I know from my time as a **big shot in oil** that its tough to find these days on accounta I sure as hell couldnt find any in **Texas**

71

Since the nine asians was **actin floppy** on war with ol Saddam we had to act fast on accounta the real **hot weather** was comin so we had to invade while the **air conditionin** still worked and we couldnt invade without a **nine asians resolution** which is some kinda evil diploshit since there was already a resolution tellin Saddam to **git outa araq** or have his ass whipped so thats what we did

Liberal **peaceniks** was actually callin Primester Tony Blair a **dawg** which is just evil on accounta he **aint no dawg**. He is a man of cacter and curge who I am proud to call my fren and I wouldnt say that about no dawg which I know on accounta I already have **two dawgs** that dont look **nothin like** Primester Blair

'Sympathy' AFTER BRITON RIVIÈRE ©Steve Bell 2003·1875·31·1·

75

In these days of surgical strikes and **smart bombs** goin to war is more and more like a visit from a popular **TV physician** like Doctor Kildare or Marcus Welby MD. The only difference is theres a helluva lot **more hardware** to haul around and we do **preemptive callouts**

A few **chickenshit states** in the nine asians like France Germany Russia and China was actin even more chickenshit than ever so we put our own collition together to **attack araq** with some tougher states like Lithedonia Boswegia Slokraine and **goon island** in the pacific

77

When you gotta go **you gotta go** so when the time came I rang up our **stonch ally** Primester Tony Blair and told him wed gone already. I always like talkin with Tony as hes my fren and when he says somethin its like **its the right thing** and he **really believes it** too so when he said he was narrowin his eyes on accounta we was at war I gotta real warm feelin like we was **family** and he didnt cut up that I wasnt tellin him first on accounta technically hes a **communist**

The other thing about tellin primester Tony Blair things is that whenever you tell him stuff he has to go **tell the Queen** on accounta thats how it works over there. She told the wurl that she was givin **Belgium** a miss that week which was kinda a giveaway on accounta everone knows Belgium is fulla **terrsts** on accounta its where the **yurpeen union** is holed up

Primester Blair also has **tell the parlment** which is like fulla **communists** who mostly do what they is told but sometimes need **leanin on** a little. One of his own **govermint guys** started actin up but he was **too short** and **too ugly** to make too much difference to the vote

Another of his govermint guys was a big ugly **communist broad** who started actin up but then Primester Tony Blair won her over by the force of his personal charm so we was **all set**

© Steve Bell 2003 ~ 1895 · 19 · 3 · 03 -

81

Just like Poppy done back in **91** I announced to the waitin wurl from the **oval orifice** that we was goin in **strong and hard**. One of our operatives got the idea of **shock and awe** from a fortune cookie and thats how we played it. First comes **shock** which is like really big bangs like youve never heard before then comes **awe** which is like ol Saddam sayin – Awe Ive **crapped my pants!**

Like in Fanistan I wanted the **first bombs to be food** but then it all started movin too fast for any of that so we drove in on accounta the **shock and awe** was workin its magic tricks an ol Saddams crack troops was **disappearin** like mist off a cows ass

There was a lotta defeatist liberal crap about **cladral damage** which is what happens when pain in the ass innocent bystanders ignore the shock and the awe and git in the way of the **crossfire**. There was some real sick pictures goin out on some of the airb TV stations which kinda tells you a lot about **how sick** those people is. The US channels showed a little more **respec**

The other sick thing was people makin out we didn have no **innational authordy** to do what had to be done to git ol Saddam which was one big crock of dirty lies as we had **Reslutionfourteenfordythreeohtwo** plus the Boswegians and the Slokrainians and the goon islanders promisin help down the line plus the Britishers on the ground and the spanecians comin up the rear. There may even have been some canadians like I give a shit

Some araqis didnt follow the collitions **simple instructions** to stay indoors dont go upstairs dont go downstairs dont drink the **water** dont go shoppin leave yur car in the **garage** and dont drive anywhere then they wonder why some of em git **caught in crossfire**

We had a shitload of **araqi exles** tellin us what to do and where to go to find dubyemdee in araq and then they was gonna take over **runnin araq** while we looked after ther oil for em after we brung em **freeman moxy**. The main guy was **charlieB** who we had fixed to take over as **head honcho**. Turns out he hadnt been in araq since he was twelve which meant the araqis thought he was somebody else an they **laughed at him** so it was all gonna take longer than we thought

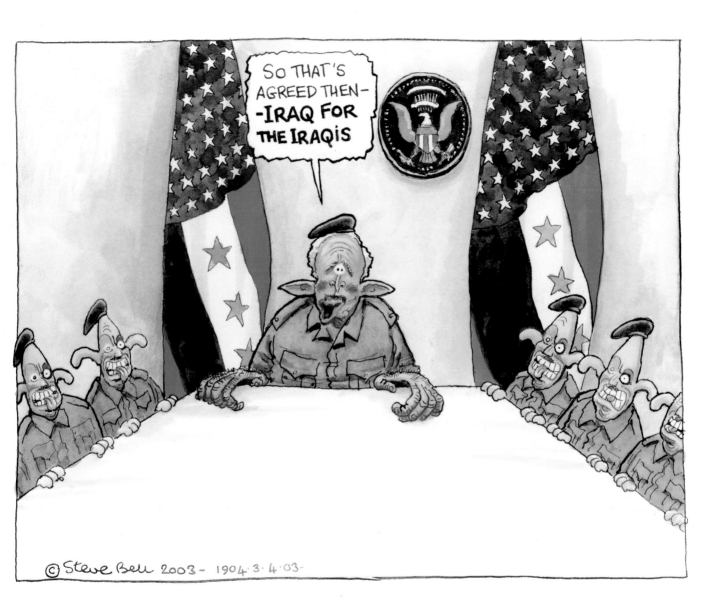

Primester Tony Blair wanted the **nine asians involved** to kinda **cover his ass** with the britisher communist party and the liberal peaceniks and I told him he was **wastin his time** with that bunch of evildoers but he didn listen. Tonys trick is he **believes** everthing he says when hes saying it but once hes said it things kinda **change** so you gotta kinda **go along with it** and make out you believe it too then hes happy so I said yeah **bring em on board**. Like my ass

93

We got to **Baghdad** real fast. Our boys punched clean into the middle of town and there was no resistance except from some guys from **airb cable** who was from **outa town**

The rest is **history** which is kinda where I **lose interest**. The entire araqi people forgot about cladral damage and shit like that an **rose up** and thanked our boys then pulled down that **statue of ol Saddam** with ther bare hands plus a little help from one of our special **crane tanks** who just happened to be around on accounta modern warfare is a lot about knockin things down then pullin em up again. Primester Tony Blair was **real pleased** as it kinda upstaged his main rival for the britisher communist leadership the evil fat finance guy **Gorn Brown**

It was just like beatin **the most evil guy in the wurl ever** and it made the cover of time magazine. Ol Saddam **disappeared** and his evil regime an all which meant that a few windows got broke and some TVs stolen which was **only natral** like Rummy said at the time

Now was the time to bring the **freeman moxy** but first we had to make sure the gas was flowin on accounta you dont git no freeman moxy if you aint prepared to **pay for it** with **blood treasure and oil** like jesus told me

The britishers have a **communist healthcare system** which is a outrage to any frenna freem on accounta it costs em **a arm an a leg** which is money they could be spendin on **defense**. Primester Tony Blair knows this is wrong so he wants to **reform it** by bringin in some proper expertise like Halliburton and **Jarvis** which is kinda like a britisher halliburton

99

The other thing that keeps my fren Tony awake nights is **xylophone seekers** comin outa the drains and threatnin his children on accounta they wanna come over and **flood the communist healthcare system** with ther shitty unhygienic lifestyles

Now we had **won the worn araq** it was time to git back to the **worn turrrsm** which never ends. Osama Bin Laden was still on holiday accordin to our best intelligence so we had to find a **new threat** which turned out to be **forn terrrsts** with links to **Algator** comin to araq and playin hell with our **buildin freeman moxy**

I was **real proud** when the nine asians said – **OK mercas in charge in araq now** since they didn really have no choice on accounta we was there and they wasnt. So now it was time to bring freeman moxy once we got the oil flowin and stopped the **fnacle moozlum clerks** attackin freem and underminin moxy

© Steve Bell 2003 - 1928. 23.5.03~

Now I was able to give my full attention to **the roadmap**. The way I see it we gotta have the **jews in Isreal** on accounta its written that if we dont got the jews there then we aint gonna git **the rapture** which is where **gods chosen** get to fly up to heaven and git to sit at the **right handa jesus** with the **lambs** and the non smokers but **not the jews** on accounta they bumped off jesus and as for the **policed injuns** – what do you expect from folks who **wear tablecloths** and blow emselves to **shit**? They only got emselves to blame

Turns out **not everbody** in Isreal liked the roadmap. The policed injuns kept blowin emselves to shit after **Areal Shroan** targeted some **terrrst killers** who like to hang out in civilian areas. But these is kinda like **folds in the roadmap** which is to be expected so it didn worry me too bad

Back in araq some o the **natral high spirits** of the newly free araqi people was gettin outa hand they was doin more than breakin windows an stealin TVs an bein like terrrsts which is **looters**. We had a **plan** for postwar araq which was to **find dubyemdee** only we hadnt found any yet which I thought was real honest of us on accounta we coulda **made up** findin dubyemdee and nobody woulda **knowed any different** but they mighta suspected

So then it comes to a lotta **liberal bleatin** about **dossiers** which didn concern me too much on accounta I always thought dossier was somethin women wear to keep ther tits from fallin out but for primester Tony Blair it was **different**. A dossier is what the britishers use to put ther **intelligence** in so its like a big bundle o paper only his turns out to be **fulla shit**

In araq there was **terrrsts** and **looters** and there was also **rump splinner groups** that was loyal to ol Saddam plus **fnacle moozlum clerks** and a shitload o **shiites** who was supposed to be in the majordy but dont do nothin without bein told to by a fnacle moozlum clerk. Everbody wants **freeman moxy** but we dont want no shiites votin in no fnacle moozlum clerk so these things take time and some of our boys was **gittin whacked** on a regular basis but I wont make no reference to it on accounta I got **too much respec** for ther loss

Then in a move led by forners from outa town **suicidal terrrst splinner looters** hit the **nine asians compound** and then the chickenshit nine asians said – we gotta git outa here on accounta there **aint no securdy**. This is plain wrong on accounta securdy is our **first priordy** only the forn looter splinner terrrsts is tryin to make out it aint

My fren Tony was havin problems provin that his **intelligence** was good when one o his **intelligence guys** bumped himself off on accounta he told some guy in the **BBC** that Primester Blair **had sex** with his dossier. The BBC is like the **CIA** only its british and they dont carry ads

Primester Blair was in **deep shit** on accounta they had to have an **inkery** with a judge an all into why this dead guy popped himself. It made Primester Blair **look kinda bad** but fortunately there was a guy called **hoon** that looked even worse so it took some of the **heat off**

Labor day come around as usual which is when I dress up to look like a worker instead of a **commander in chief** which is what I am on accounta I dont have to **explain myself** to nobody. There was talk about **dead troops** but I dont hold with any o that as I got too much **respec**

113

So when the commander in chief goes to **congress** to ask for the finance for **doin up araq** they all jump and gimme what I want otherwise they end up lookin like **traitorous pieces o shit**

The nine asians dont see things in the same way an talk up some **critical crap** about the mercan forces in araq. These folks sit there in New York take our money then have no idea of **whats unmercan** and whats not. **Most of the nine asians** turn out to be unmercan which explains a lotta whats wrong with the wurl today

115

Then its the anniversary of the **first dossier** like I give a shit. Primester Blair called this the **darjeeling dossier** on accounta its not his cuppa tea. There was some real **crapola intelligence** put in there like Saddam coulda blown off a **innercannibalistic missle** inside **45 seconds** which it turns out was put there by hired comedians which our **CIA guys** told em at the time

Then some **forn fananimalist fnadic moozlum suicide splinner rump elements** tried to blow up Rummys number two **wolfie** who was on holiday in araq at the time. This was startin to get **personal**

Pretty soon our dead guys started **comin home** from araq so I made sure they got **plenty respec** and was **left alone by the media** so ther familys would be left in peace and not waste time answerin no tasteless questions from people with **no respec**

119

We was already buildin up a **big war chest** for the 2004 election campaign in fact we was doin better than our **wildest dreams**. This was not just on accounta little ol ladies givin us a **coupla dollars** though that kinda small time stuff is always **kinda humblin** to receive. Where we was makin big breakthroughs was with the **corporations** who was all comin across for us when they see us **deliver on our promises** which is what politics oughta be about

THEY SHALL NOT GROW RICH, AS WE THAT SENT THEM THERE GROW RICH
THEY SHALL NOT PLEDGE CASH, NOR THEIR VOTES COUNT THEM
AT THE RAISING OF THE FUNDS AND AT THE LUNCHEONS
WE WILL FORGET THE DEAD AND REMEMBER HALLIBURTON

When people say we didn have no clear **postwar plan** they know ther talkin so much shit on accounta we been plannin to **git out quick** from before even we went in. We mercans is not about **empire buildin** all we wanna do is bring **freeman moxy** and then get the hell out and we especially aint innerested in no **oil**

In november myself and Laura came over to **visit with my fren** Primester Tony Blair an his lovely wife **Cherokee** and **stay with the Queen** in her London palace home. This is a **great honour** on accounta visiting presidents usually gotta stay **up town** next door to the **zoo** and spend nights listenin to the wolfs howlin and the chimps a screechin an I need my beauty sleep

123

Then I made a surprise trip to **visit with our boys in araq** for thanksgiving when I brung em a big fiberglass **turkey** which looked great for the cameras but didn taste so good on accounta the **real thing** comes presliced and flown in from home in a box and this was just for show but **no bastard told me**

Then our boys found **ol Saddam** hidin in a hidey hole which was my **best christmas present ever**. Our doctors checked him out for **DNA** an facial hair on accounta the guy had a lotta doubles runnin around who coulda been anybody

125

Then comes the **questions** – what is you gonna **do with him** which I dont hafta explain on accounta Im **commander in chief** so they just gotta guess for now

Then I had another **great idea** an this was a real **big one**. We done Fanistan we done araq why dont we **do space the final frontier**? Lets go to **Mars** gentlemen we have the technology we have **mercan knowhow** and the mercan people wanna be inspired on accounta they is fed up with a diet of **gameshows** and **reality TV** and too much **cheap farmed fish** and I know the human bein and fish can **coexist peacefully** specially on Mars

Folks say Im kinda like **John F Kennedy** except he was a **democrat** that fucked everthing that moved and I am a **republican** that remain **faithful** to my lovely wife Condolaura and is pledged **never** to have sex in the **oval orifice**. Apart from that we is both aimin to **conquer space the final frontier** and plant the **mercan flag** where it aint never been planted before

129

The top judge runnin the **inkery** that had been lookin into my fren Tony Blairs **darjeeling dossier** found that **everbody was guilty** except for Primester Blair and that the **BBC** was **chock fulla evildoers** that needed to be dealt with **pronto**. I rang Tony to say way to go an then I rung the judge who was called Lauren Hutton and told him he could hold a inkery into me **anytime he wanted** an thered be good money in it

Even after **that** the liberal shitheads and peaceniks was still gripin about **dubyemdee**. Does nobody **learn nothin** in this business? When a **top judge** says there was **no talkin up dubyemdee** an that Primester Blair never had **no sex with no dossier** that means we is innocent on accounta there might have been some shit talked about dubyemdee but we **didn know any better**

133

The **fananimalist fnadics** at the **BBC** was still puttin it out that Lauren Huttons inkery was a **whitewash** and primester Blair was a evil lyin piece o shit on accounta they had **mind control** over the entire britisher people which is a bit like the liberal media mind control over here except we got **Fox** and **Rush Limbaugh** to balance things out. They just got evildoers spoutin **unmercan lies** all day everday

Then they is complainin about Saddams **45 second innercannibalistic missles** crapola which they say say was a plain lie but we know was **secure intelligence** on accounta what our CIA guys was talkin about was not **strategical** 45 second innercannibalistic missles at all but **battlefield** 45 second innercannibalistic missles which is a different thing

135

Meanwhile my fren Tony was workin on some kinda **diplocrap** on accounta he **enjoys** that kinda thing. Turns out hes gotta the evil terrrst from Libya **Criminal Gadaffy** to stop bein a evildoer. This guy was **number one wurl evildoer** back when Poppy was veep to Reagan so this is a pretty darn big thing an I wouldn touch the guy with a bargepole myself on accounta him bein so evil but Tony says he likes uncle dollar an hes got **plenty oil** which means the **worn turrrism** is really workin since he wouldna **stopped bein evil** if we hadna beat Saddam into a **rat shit** an anyway we already blew his daughter away back in **86**

The election is hottin up so it looks like the democrats is gonna choose a flop haired pointy headed **liberal peacenik** who just happened to be a **war hero** back in Vitnam like big deal Im shittin my pants already as if I got problems with my own war record **which I dont**. I did what I had to I learned to **fly a airplane** an all for my country so I didn get shot an **come home in a box** is this some kinda **crime**?

My **big pitch** for the election besides bein a **successful war leader** is Im gonna **stop homos havin weddins** on accounta it aint natral an jesus would be turnin on his cross if he heard about it. Like when I think o two guys givin it each other **up the ass** then goin a church an expectin the minister not to **puke all over em** I think its wrong an Im pretty darn sure the **mercan people** agree with me on this one

139

Among the hundreds **evildoers and terrrsts** we was holdin in **camp x-ray** which is in cuba on accounta it would be **illegal** in the nicedaysmerca there is one or two maybe five britishers who we let go back to **britisher land** on accounta if we aint got nothin outa them in two years they is either nuts or they is somebody else. They was defnaly guilty though as we got **intelligence** that tells us this only it is secret

141

Then **algator** decides to hit some **spanecian trains** in the mornin rush hour. Spanecia is a **backward country** where folks still travel by train and they is also a major part of the **collition** after primester Blair and its got **troops in araq** alongside the povenians and the slokrainians. **Primester aznar** who is **my fren** an was runnin for election at the time tried to pin it on the local **spanecian terrrsts** who wear womens undergarments but the spanecians knowed it was **algator** on accounta it was done too early in the day for spanecians who like doin things **manana**

So the communists got voted in who said they was gonna **pull out the spanecian troops** from araq which was a terble thing

143

Back home there was another **inkery** into what happened at **911** but the mercan constitution says the commander in chief dont hafta explain himself to **nobody about nothin no time**. Condi tells em this but they say we done **diddlysquat** about about terrrsm until 911 on accounta we was **obsessed about araq** so she says shell **testify** an shes one fine lookin broad who speaks **real good english** and nobody was none the wiser on accounta she didn tell em anything so I asked her if shed marry me on accounta Im thinkin about **turnin mormon**

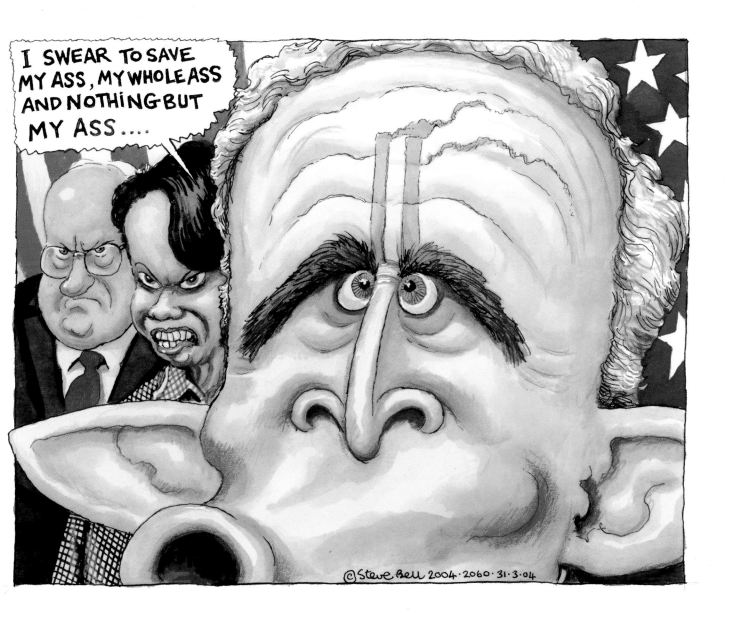

In araq **violence** was startin to break out led by **floojan forn fnadics surgeons** an **renegade shiite moozlum clerks**. They chopped up some **civilian securdy guys** an hung em on a bridge an took pictures so we wasnt gonna let that one go on accounta theres one thing **we wont stand** which is folks who dont show the dead **no respec**. Flooja was gonna be hearin from us **real soon**

147

This didn affect our plans to **hand over soverdy** to the araqis on June 30th on accounta though we is handin over **soverdy** we is keepin controla **securdy** an helpin em **pump oil** an stuff

Turns out they is a **few more fnadics** in flooja than we thought who **hang out in mosques** on accounta they is also **slamic fananimalists** so they shouldn be too surprised when we whack a coupla mosques an put snipers in a coupla others on accounta we gotta **do whats gotta be done** otherwise we gonna look like chickenshit wuss **walkovers**

151

Rummy forgot to tell me that some damn **trailer trash** runnin **ali booger jailhouse** was treatin airb suspec fnadic splinner rump fananimalist Saddam loyalist terrrsts **like dawgs** then takin **pictures** so I gotta go on **airb TV** an make some kinda apology on accounta all the airbs in the mideast is **foamin at the mouth** on accounta they dont know no better so its kinda **necessary diplocrap**

153

Sayin we treatin **suspec airb splinner rump suicide terrrsts** like **dawgs** is one o the stupidest things I ever heard on accounta that for the kinda **trailer trash** we put in charge o **ali booger jailhouse** eatin dawgfood is **normal** an bein treated like a dawg is a **step up in the wurl**

When you gotta do whats gotta be done you gotta **pay what it costs** which is a lotta dollars an a lotta **brave guys** that might end up dead but if you **dont** do whats gotta be done then the chances are that sombody else is gonna **do it to you** only **worse**. That would be like **givin in** to the bad guys the guys with facial hair ol Saddams guys the **remnants** the **splinner leftovers** the **surgeons** the **fananimalist forn fnadics** who **hate freeman moxy** and **love terrr**. You is either on one side or the other in this war you caint pick n choose you is **against evil** or you is **for it** so which is it to be?

Glossary of useful words and phrases

Airbs	Folks who is mainly moozlums
Algator	International terrrst organisation
Araq	Big oil producer run by major league evildoer Saddam Hussein
Araqi exles	Folks from araq who live in the Nicedaysmerca and believe in the noomercansentry like CharlieB
Areal Shroan	Primester of Isreal
Axle of Elvis	Where evildoers breed
Boswegia	Somewhere in eastern yurp
Boswegian	Inhabitant of Boswegia
Cacter	What Bill Clinton lacks
CharlieB	Araqi exle and future head honcho of araq
Cladral damage	What happens to pain in the ass inocent bystanders that dont keep ther heads down
Collition	Alliance against terrrsm and Saddam Hussein. Mainly britishers plus some Boswegians and Slokrainians and goonislanders
Crossfire	What mercan troops produce
Curge	You gotta show whos got the biggest. If you dont got it yur chickenshit
Diplocrap	Talkin to forners
Dubya	My nickname after my great grandaddy Herbert Wokker who raised the finance for the fewer
Enronistan	Evildoer state out east
Evildoer	Anyone who is not a frenna freem
Evelyn Tent	What evildoers have
Fanistan	Evil turrrst state run by the television who harbored Algator

Fewer	Chancellor and head honcho of germany 1933–1945
Floojans	Inhabitants of Flooja mostly forn terrrsts
Forn	From abroad
Forn fnadics	Fananimalist moozlums from abroad
Forn policy	Mainly involves diplocrap. Mine is strictly forn handed
Forner	Inhabitant of abroad
Fornfiders	Inhabitants from abroad carryin guns
Fratboy	Young folk with hard drinkin hard snortin lifestyle
Freeman moxy	Mercas gif to the wurl
Frenna Freem	Anyone who is not a evildoer
Global wurl	Where Halliburton operates
Hungrovia	Somewhere in central yurp
Innational authordy	The Nicedaysmerca
Inkery	Official fact findin whitewash
Isreal	Promised Land of the Roadmap
Lithedonia	Somewhere in eastern yurp
Merca	The finest country in the wurl of which I am proud to be president
Mercan People	Jack and Hortense who live in a cupboard in the oval orifice
Morls	Things that stop you havin blowjobs in the oval orifice. If you dont have these you aint fit to be president
Morl curge	What you need to be a wurl class wurl leader
Moozlums	Folks who is mainly airbs
Mogdadalsadr	Fnacle moozlum clerk
Neecon	Folks who believe in the Noomercansentry incorporatin jews fer jesus
Nicedaysmerca	Full name of the finest country in the wurl of which I am proud to be president
Nine asians	Organisation of evildoers

Noomercansentry	The future of our wurl
Nornlions	Pro western rebels in Fanistan who hate the television
Osama Bin Laden	Old Bush family friend
Policed injuns	Illegal inhabitants of isreal
Povenia	Somewhere in eastern yurp
Primester	Head honcho but smaller cheese than a president
Roadmap	Plan for wherever Areal Shroan wants to go to process peace
Rudovia	Somewhere in central eastern yurp
Slamic fananimalism	What moozlum fnadics believe in
Slokraine	Somewhere in eastern central yurp
Steel Turrfs	Helpin me get reelected in rustybelt states
Surgeons	Illegal araqi terrrsts tryin to overthrow freeman moxy
Television	Fnacle moozlums who ran Fanistan
Terrrsm	What terrrsts git up to
Terrrsts	Folks who perform acts of terrrsm
Turrfs	Barriers to trade which fuck up the global wurl
Turrrism	Same as terrrsm only spelt different
Veep	Dick Cheney my number two
Worn turrrsm	It never ends
Wurl	Where aliens invade
WMD	Dubyemdee. What I woulda been called if Id a been a doctor
Xylophone Seekers	What keeps Primester Tony Blair awake nights
Yellowcake	Follow the Yellowcake road to find the Dubyemdee
Yurp	Continent above Africa and to the left of Asia
Yurpeens	People of yurp
Yurpeen Union	Another organisation of evildoers